This journal belongs to

_____

Jesus Is Mine

COMFORT DEVOTIONAL JOURNAL

BELLE
CITY
GIFTS

Belle City Gifts
Racine, Wisconsin, USA

Belle City Gifts is an imprint of BroadStreet Publishing Group LLC.
Broadstreetpublishing.com

Jesus Is Mine: COMFORT DEVOTIONAL JOURNAL

ISBN 978-1-4245-5059-3

Devotional entries composed by Shannon Lindsay, Michelle Winger, and Deb Wyss.

Design by Chris Garborg | www.garborgdesign.com
Editorial services by Michelle Winger | www.literallyprecise.com

Printed in China.

15   16   17   18   19   20   21   7   6   5   4   3   2   1

May our Lord Jesus Christ himself and God our Father, who loved us and by his grace gave us eternal comfort and a wonderful hope, comfort you and strengthen you.

2 THESSALONIANS 2:16-17 NLT

Introduction

The circumstances of life can take us through
seasons of grief, anxiety, loss, discouragement,
and difficulty. This devotional journal is filled
with comforting messages of hope and
encouragement for when you find yourself in
challenging situations. Let each entry speak
to the depth of your heart, showing you how
much you are loved and understood by the one
who is always near. Take some time to express
your thoughts and emotions in the journaling
space provided, and be encouraged as you
spend time with God. He is your true source of
comfort for every day.

He Makes All Things Possible

It is God who makes us able to do all that we do.

2 Corinthians 12:9 ESV

In the midst of trying situations, there are days when we're so exhausted we feel like we can barely put one foot in front of the other. The thought of creating some semblance of a meal, or even getting out of bed for that matter, seems near impossible. Forget about responding gracefully when people say or do ridiculous things. Forget about the project that was supposed to be finished two weeks ago. Forget about going to that event we thought we wanted to attend. We just *can't* keep up.

The good news is God doesn't expect us to. In fact, he doesn't even want us to. His power is made perfect in our weakness. Our *weakness*. When we allow ourselves to be weak in our grief-filled moments, we give God the opportunity to show his strength—and he'll take that opportunity every time we give it to him. We don't have to be "willing and able"; we can just be "willing" because *God* is able.

What tasks seem impossible to you today? Let God rest on you in your weakness. Ask him to give you the strength you need to either do the things that have to get done, or to say no to the things that can wait. He will make you able if you are willing.

He Accepts Me

Long ago, even before he made the world, God chose us to be his very own through what Christ would do for us; he decided then to make us holy in his eyes, without a single fault—we who stand before him covered with his love.

Ephesians 1:4 TLB

Applications are essential for gleaning the promising applicants from the inadequate. Fill out this form, and find out if you're approved for a home loan, for college admittance, for a credit card. We put our best qualities on paper, tweak our weaknesses, and hope for approval. But rejection is always a possibility.

With God, however, our acceptance has already been promised. We must only appeal to his son Jesus, who steps in on our behalf and petitions for our approval. There is no credit flaw, no failing grade, and no past default that his death on the cross doesn't redeem completely. Because we are covered with his loving forgiveness, there is no flaw in us. We are accepted by God as part of his family and redeemed by his grace for his eternal kingdom.

Can you believe your acceptance? Stand on the promise that there is nothing in your history—no past or present sin—that can separate you from his love. Cast everything upon him and have faith; you are wholly accepted and abundantly loved!

He Is My Father

But when the right time came, God sent his Son, born of a woman,
subject to the law. God sent him to buy freedom for us who were slaves
to the law, so that he could adopt us as his very own children.

Galatians 4:4-5 NLT

Once upon a time, a courtyard in a faraway land overflowed with lost children.
They were all very dirty, dressed in threadbare garments, and deeply hungry.
Some children had gaping wounds, others were bruised or limping. A man
walked among them, gently tending to their needs.

Next to the courtyard was a majestic castle with bright flags and high winding
turrets. The doors of the castle were wide open, and inside was a banquet with
delicious food, warm fires, and robes of velvet. A king sat inside, surrounded by
his children who were clean, fed, and smiling. He looked out over the courtyard
with longing.

Two children approached the doorway, smelling the food and feeling the warmth
from the castle. The man in the courtyard took their hands and asked if they
would like to join the king as his children. One leaped for joy, and, not waiting
another second, ran into the castle. The other held back, looked down at her
filthy rags, and shook her head. She wandered back amongst the other children.

Daughter, are you wandering in the courtyard? Why do you believe that
your sins make you unworthy of God's banquet? You have been bought
at a high price and are adopted into the family of God. He is your Father,
and he offers the only cleansing redemption you need.

He Is My Assurance

"I know that my Redeemer lives,
and he will stand upon the earth at last.
And after my body has decayed,
yet in my body I will see God! I will see him for myself.
Yes, I will see him with my own eyes.
I am overwhelmed at the thought!"

Job 19:25-27 NLT

In a matter of days, everything was destroyed. First his 11,000 livestock and servants were stolen, burned, or killed. Then his ten children were all killed at once. To make matters worse, this unfortunate man's skin was plagued with painful sores, which he scraped off with a piece of broken pottery.

How could anyone endure such tragedy? To be fair, Job mourns, and laments, and weeps. He is confused, hopeless, and weak. On top of feeling cursed and desperate, he is taunted by his friends and wife: Give up on God; he has given up on you! Stop waiting on God to redeem you; he has obviously forgotten you! But Job refuses to curse God, as God knew he would, and despite the tragedies he endured, Job is assured that God will not fail when it matters most.

Job's faith has been weakened by the test, but he clutches desperately to the one promise that can sustain him: no matter what happens to Job in his earth-bound life, nothing can take away the joy he will share with God in his eternal life.

Everything on earth is a fleeting treasure, a momentary comfort that can be lost in a flash. But the assurance of your eternal place in his kingdom, if you have submitted your life to Jesus Christ, is indestructible. How does this bring you comfort today?

He Is Real

His divine power has given us everything we need for a godly life through our knowledge of him who called us by his own glory and goodness. Through these he has given us his very great and precious promises, so that through them you may participate in the divine nature, having escaped the corruption in the world caused by evil desires.

2 Peter 1:3-4 NIV

The test for authenticity is often measured by applying some kind of force or foreign substance to that which is being tested. Determining whether something is made of real gold can be accomplished in a number of ways. Perhaps the most simple is by rubbing the gold on an unglazed ceramic plate. The color of the mark left on the plate determines the authenticity of the gold. Real gold will leave a gold mark. Fake gold will leave a black mark. You can see the analogy, can't you?

At some time in our lives, we will undergo an authenticity test. We might be put through several—daily. What mark will we leave when we encounter those tests? When we brush up against difficulty? If we are authentic Christians, the mark we leave will be gold—the true mark of Christ. Unfortunately, black marks and scars cover many who have been hurt by fakes.

God is real, and he is good. He has given us an example of how to remain authentic in a world full of fraud and deception. If you have been hurt by someone you thought was being real with you, you are not alone. Remember God's great and precious promises today, and press on in his strength.

How can you continue to leave an authentic mark of gold when you brush up against difficult situations?

He Blesses Me

"My heart rejoices in the LORD!
The Lord has made me strong.
Now I have an answer for my enemies;
I rejoice because you rescued me.
No one is holy like the Lord!
There is no one besides you;
there is no Rock like our God."

1 Samuel 2:1-2 NLT

Consider for a moment the most joyous time of your walk with Christ. Imagine the delight of that season, the lightness and pleasure in your heart. Rest in the memory for a minute, and let the emotions come back to you. Is the joy returning? Do you feel it? Now, hear this truth: The way you felt about God at the highest, most joyful, amazing, glorious moment is how he feels about you *at all times!*

What a glorious blessing! Our joy is an overflow of his heart's joy toward us; it is just one of the many blessings God showers over us. When we realize how good he is, and that he has granted us everything we need for salvation through Jesus, we can rejoice!

The season of your greatest rejoicing can be now, when you consider the strength he provides, the suffering from which you have been rescued, and the rock that is our God. His blessings don't depend on our feeling joyous; we experience joy because we realize God's gracious and loving blessings.

Lift your praises to him and let your song be never-ending. Relive the season of blessing each and every day!

He Gives Me Boldness

So let us come boldly to the throne of our gracious God. There we will
receive his mercy, and we will find grace to help us when we need it most.

Hebrews 4:16 NLT

Imagine walking into Buckingham Palace, unnoticed and unrestricted, without knocking or announcing yourself, and pulling up a chair alongside Her Majesty, the Queen of England. "I've had such a long day. Nothing has gone right, and now my car is making the strangest noise. Could you help me out?"

Such an image is almost absurd! There is a protocol to seeing royalty—many rules to follow, not to mention the armed guards protecting every side. But there is a royal throne we can approach without fear or proper etiquette. It is without guards, payments, locks, and restrictions. Its occupant is the God of all creation, and he is eager to hear about your day's ups and downs.

Approach the throne, shamelessly pull up a chair, and lift your voice to
him. He loves your company. What do you need? Ask him without fear.
What gifts has he given? Thank him in person. What guidance are you
looking for? His wisdom is yours if you will listen.

He Is My Comfort

To all who mourn... he will give: beauty for ashes; joy instead of mourning; praise instead of heaviness. For God has planted them like strong and graceful oaks for his own glory.

Isaiah 61:3 TLB

How many thoughts does the human brain conceive in an hour? In a day? In a lifetime? How many of those thoughts are about God: who he is and what he has done for his children? Imagine your own thoughts about life—grocery lists, dentist appointments, song lyrics, lost keys—and your thoughts about God—his majesty, holiness, comfort, creativity—weighed against each other on a scale. Likely, it would tip in favor of the many details of human existence.

These temporary details overshadow the one comfort and promise we can rely on: the gospel of Jesus' birth, death, resurrection, and ascension for our eternal salvation. Wipe every other thought away and we are left with this truth. For those burdened by their sin it is of great comfort! Jesus came to give us new life!

You are not a weak sapling, limited by inadequate light and meager nourishment. You are a strong and graceful oak, soaring and resilient for the glory of God. Ashes and mourning and heavy burdens are relieved. The scales tip to this one weighty thought: you are his.

Let your thoughts stretch above the canopy of everyday human details to bask in this joy: he has given you everything you need in Jesus. How does this thought bring you relief today?

He Is Compassionate

The L{ORD} is compassionate and gracious,
Slow to anger and abounding in lovingkindness.

Psalm 103:8 NASB

Consider the Israelites wandering in the desert: God had rescued them out of bondage and goes before them in a pillar of fire, providing for their every need and protecting them. What do they offer to him? Complaints.

Listen to the psalms of David—the man after God's own heart—as he lays his burdens at the feet of God, praising his majesty and might. But what does David do when he wants what he cannot have? Steals, murders, and lies.

Paul, who gave his life to preach the gospel he loved to people near and far, shares the astounding gift of God's grace to Jews and Gentiles alike. But who was he before his conversion? A hateful, persecuting murderer of Christians.

God loves his children regardless of their sin, their past, and their failings. This love is poured out on us with consideration and patience. We aren't dealt with as we deserve; rather, according to his great love for us. Can we say the same about how we treat those around us? Are we compassionate, slow to anger, and full of love? Or are we offended, impatient, and aggravated?

Determine if you have sinned in this way, repent, and then rejoice!
God has compassion for you. You are forgiven and he loves you with
abundance! How does this change the way you go about the day?

He Calms My Heart

When you go through deep waters and great trouble, I will be with you.
When you go through rivers of difficulty, you will not drown! When you
walk through the fire of oppression, you will not be burned up—the
flames will not consume you.

Isaiah 43:2 TLB

When the hospital doors slide open and we aren't sure what news will greet us, God is compassionate. When the boss calls us for a meeting and dismissal is a real possibility, God is gentle. When we return home late at night to find our personal treasures stolen or destroyed, God is comforting. He cares so deeply for us.

Some see God as distant, vengeful, or condemning. Others see God as kind, affectionate, and attentive. Sometimes circumstances become too overwhelming. Mountains of anxiety rise up and we feel isolated and alone.

Let no doubt take root; he is a God who cares deeply, loves fully, and remains faithful, ever at our side in times of trouble. Though our sorrows overwhelm us, he is the comfort that we need.

Will you take his hand, offered in love, and receive his comforting touch? Will you remember his faithfulness and let it calm your heart? He is with you! You will not drown! The flames will not consume you! Cling to his promises, and the mountains, as high as they may seem, will crumble at your feet.

Which mountains of difficulty do you need to see crumble in your life today?

He Gives Me Confidence

"For my thoughts are not your thoughts,
*neither are your ways my ways, declares the L*ORD*.*
For as the heavens are higher than the earth,
so are my ways higher than your ways
and my thoughts than your thoughts."

Isaiah 55:8-9 E SV

In times of war, army strategists benefit from high vantage points. Looking upon the battlefield from above is the best way to formulate strategies for their troops. Before the use of satellite equipment and heat-sensing radar, views were limited to ground level, forcing strategists to use whatever maps and spies they could to predict enemy movement and position their men.

In the same way, our lives benefit from a higher viewpoint. When we rise above our circumstances and see life not from our own anxious, urgent, overwhelming perspective but from God's, life's battles become less intimidating as eternity's promises rise into view.

God has plans for our lives, but sometimes they are hard to see. The day-to-day defeats of life consume us and we struggle to confidently lift our head above the fray. When this happens, we can remember his high thoughts and ways, and believe that he will lead us through. He can see the entire battlefield, when we can only see our private foxhole and the crushing explosions that surround us.

What does it look like for you to trust God in the battle today? You can
be confident that he will lead you safely to victory.

He Lifts Me Up

You, O Lord, are a shield about me,
My glory, and the One who lifts my head.

Psalm 3:3 NASB

Picture a young girl running a race. She leaps off to a great start when the gun sounds. She pushes her way to the front of the pack in no time and sets a pace that is tough to compete with. As she rounds the final corner with the finish line in sight, she stumbles. She tries desperately to regain her balance, but it's too late. She crashes to the ground. Trying to be brave, she jumps up and sprints the final yards to complete the race. Fourth place.

Head hung low, skinned knees burning, and vision blurry, she walks over to her coach. He gently lifts her chin to the sun, and brushes away the tears that have spilled over. As her bottom lip begins to quiver, he reassures her that everything is going to be ok. That life is full of painful moments that creep up unexpectedly, but it's also full of second chances. "Don't give up on yourself," he says, "I haven't given up on you."

When we've given up, run away, lost the plot, or stumbled and fallen, God doesn't give up on us. When we come to him with our heads hung low, he lifts our chins, looks deep into our eyes, and whispers tender words of compassion that reach the deepest places in our hearts.

Do you feel like you can't look up? How do you think God feels about you in this moment? Let your face be tipped to the Son. Allow the words of Jesus to wash over your wounds and bring healing to your heart, soul, and mind today.

He Is All I Need

I know what it is to be in need, and I know what it is to have plenty.
I have learned the secret of being content in any and every situation,
whether well fed or hungry, whether living in plenty or in want. I can do
all this through him who gives me strength.

Philippians 4:12-13 NIV

It happens on occasion, when the heavy spring rains come, that some homeowners find themselves on hands and knees trying to staunch the flow of water into their basement. The water rushes in, not down from the walls or windows, but up from the rising water table and through the foundation. And they bow low, soaking up all that they can.

It's a trying time, to be sure, as patience wears thin and towels pile high. But remember the living water, which springs up and gives life to the full! We can remind ourselves that it is only on our knees as servants that we draw abundantly from these waters, because they rush quickly to the lowest places—places that only a humble servant can access.

It's painful at times, hard on the back and knees, to be brought so low. But the heart soars, and all your thirsts are satisfied. You are in the company of Jesus Christ, who came not to be served, but to serve. Can you think of any better place to be?

What areas of your life do you struggle to be content in? Let his living
water fill you up to overflowing with gratitude and praise.

He Gives Me Courage

I eagerly expect and hope that I will in no way be ashamed, but will have sufficient courage so that now as always Christ will be exalted in my body, whether by life or by death.

Philippians 1:20 NIV

That's a pretty strong declaration: one exemplified in the life of Vibia Perpetua, a married noblewoman and Christian martyr who died at twenty-two years of age in Third Century Rome. There is a record of her diary entries detailing her life in prison and final hours. Perpetua was arrested for her profession of faith in Christ and threatened with a harrowing execution if she did not renounce her faith. She had many compelling reasons to do just that—a nursing infant for one!

Early martyrdom wasn't only about dying for the profession of faith. It was about humiliation and torture carried out in a kind of sporting arena—with fans celebrating the demise of the victims. Yet, Perpetua displayed incredible fortitude in her final hour. Read her account and you'd have to agree that her courage could not possibly have been attributed to a human characteristic. Her courage came from God.

Having courage, being brave, remaining firm—we can only hold on for so long. Sometimes we need to recognize that it's time to call on the supernatural strength of our Father. He gives us enough courage to walk through *any* trying circumstance.

When you find yourself at the end of your courage supply, boldly ask God to replenish the stock. What are you going through today that needs a touch of supernatural courage to get through? Can you be honest with God about your need for him?

He Delights in Me

My beloved speaks and says to me:
"Arise, my love, my beautiful one,
and come away,
for behold, the winter is past;
the rain is over and gone.
The flowers appear on the earth,
the time of singing has come."

Song of Solomon 2:10-12 ESV

When we read this verse in Song of Solomon, we may feel like looking behind us for the person God is really talking to. It can be a little uncomfortable to have his gaze so intently upon us. We're nothing special, after all! Not beauty queens, academic scholars, or athletic prodigies of any kind. We might not be musical, or crafty, or organized. Our house might be a mess, and we could probably use a manicure.

Some say that romance is dead. It's not for God: the lover of our souls. He desires nothing more than time with his creation!

Do you feel a bit squeamish under such an adoring gaze? There is good news for you! You are, in fact, his beautiful one! And he does, indeed, want to bring you out of the cold winter. He's finished the watering season and it is finally—FINALLY!—time to rejoice in the season of renewal.

Why do you feel uncomfortable under the gaze of the one who loves you more than anyone else ever could? The time has come. He is calling you, regardless of how unworthy you may think you are. Will you arise and come away with your beloved? He is waiting for you!

He Is My Deliverer

I waited patiently for the LORD; he turned to me and heard my cry.
He lifted me out of the slimy pit, out of the mud and mire;
he set my feet on a rock and gave me a firm place to stand.
He put a new song in my mouth, a hymn of praise to our God.
Many will see and fear the LORD and put their trust in him.

Psalm 40:1-3 NIV

God loves us with a sacrificial love that escapes our human understanding, overwhelms our human selfishness, and humbles our human pride. Through the sacrifice of his only Son, Jesus Christ, mankind is delivered from the fate of eternal separation from God.

When we are separated, bowed low and desperate, he hears our cry. When we are forgotten and despairing, he comforts our loneliness. And when, because of our own sin, we are wicked and depraved, he cleanses us of our offensiveness and makes us suitable for glory.

God has done the impossible task of making us into something worthy of his name; he takes us from instability to security, gives us a song of praise, and makes our conversion a testimony for all creation to see. Our deliverance is an opportunity for many more to hear of his love and trust him to deliver them as well.

He has delivered you, perhaps from a pit whose depth is beyond your understanding. Be assured today that your deliverance is a miracle; it is steady and safe, and the song in your heart will be a message for many. How can you sing God's promises loud and clear today?

He Is Devoted to Me

I will sing of the LORD's great love forever;
with my mouth I will make your faithfulness known
through all generations.
I will declare that your love stands firm forever,
that you have established your faithfulness in heaven itself.

Psalm 89:1-2 NIV

God in his great power and faithfulness never fails us, never gives up on us, and will never leave us alone, out on a limb, to fend for ourselves. His love for us remains—regardless of our circumstances or our weaknesses—strong and immovable. His devotion to his children exceeds that of all parents, whose love for their children seems unmatched, but is only human. Not only does God match our love, he surpasses it. He is without limits, and nothing can ever change God's devotion.

This truth is overwhelmingly satisfying; when such devotion has been proven, what else could attract our gaze? Where else could our eyes find such beauty and purity as they do upon the face of Jesus? In awe, we recognize that his gaze is fixed right back at us, seeing us as a lovely and worthy prize. We can neither deserve this gaze nor escape it. We are flawed, but he is unwavering in his love for us.

Do you know that the Father is wholly devoted to you? Do you know
that he longs to be with you—to comfort the deepest part of you that
aches and burns? His great love for you is yours to enjoy forever. How
do you feel about his devotion toward you? Do you doubt it, or can you
accept that it is true?

He Encourages Me

The humble will see their God at work and be glad.
Let all who seek God's help be encouraged.

Psalm 69:32 NLT

"Come on!" "You can do it!" "You're almost there!" Strings of praise and faces filled with expectant wonder look on. If you were standing outside the door, you'd think someone was about to accomplish something extremely difficult. You might rush into the room to examine for yourself what momentous occasion was taking place. And you'd perhaps be perplexed at the scene in front of you. The adults in the room are crouched down on the floor looking intently at... an infant rocking back and forth on hands and knees. It's an amusing picture, but one we can learn from.

Obstacles in life come our way, and sometimes we feel like we have to figure them out all on our own. We rock forward in faith and then back as doubt creeps in. Forward again as emotions propel us, and back once more as they overwhelm. What we fail to recognize is that our Father delights in seeing us make that first move forward. He looks on in excitement as we lift an arm and then a leg. Ever encouraging, our God beckons us: Come to me. You can make it. You're almost there.

What do you need encouragement for today? Even when you feel your daunting milestone is somewhat pathetic—like moving and arm and a leg—God wants to be your constant source of encouragement. Ask for his help, and acknowledge his work in your life as you move from stalling to crawling.

He Makes All Things Beautiful

He has made everything beautiful in its time. He has also set eternity in the human heart; yet no one can fathom what God has done from beginning to end.

Ecclesiastes 3:11 NIV

We've probably all heard an older gentleman declare that his wife is more beautiful now than the day they married. And we likely thought, *He needs glasses.* What we fail to recognize in our outward-focused, airbrushed society, is that time really does make things beautiful. More accurately, time gives us better perspective on the true definition of beauty. Spending time with those we love affords us a glimpse into the depth of beauty that lies within. So while the external beauty may be fading, there is a wealth of beauty inside—*that's* what that older gentleman is referring to.

God's Word says that he makes all things beautiful in his time. *All* things. Whatever situation you are facing right now, it has the potential to create beauty in you. Perseverance, humility, grace, obedience—these are beautiful. But there's more. The beauty God creates in us cannot be fully described in human terms! There is eternal beauty to be found.

When we are met with challenges that cause us to run to God and sit in his presence, we can't help but reflect the beauty of his character. What are you facing right now that could be a catalyst for true beauty?

He Gives Me a Future

He will wipe away every tear from their eyes, and death shall be no more, neither shall there be mourning, nor crying, nor pain anymore, for the former things have passed away.

Revelation 21:4 ESV

The sin and sadness of life can make it seem like an endless night, where we are continually waiting for the dawn of Christ's return. In the darkest of nights, it doesn't always help to know that he will return *someday*, because *this day* is full of despair.

To you, his beloved daughter, he gives comfort. Don't lose heart. He is coming for you! It can be hard, because he seems to be taking a long time, but he is preparing a place for you. You are not forgotten in this long night; your pain is familiar to him. Keep your eyes fixed on him! Soon you will hear his voice! He is also longing for that moment.

We live for the promise of his return. This promise overcomes our pain, our longing, our desperation, and our limits. All things become bearable and light under the assurance of seeing Jesus, embracing him, and gazing on his beauty! We will be made into a pure and spotless bride. There is nothing more for us but to marvel at him. Glorify him. Believe him. Love him. Thank him.

How does the promise of eternity help you through your current situation?

He Gives Me Faith

Through Christ you have come to trust in God. And you have placed your faith and hope in God because he raised Christ from the dead and gave him great glory.

1 Peter 1:21 NLT

Balancing at the edge of the cliff, a climber clutches the ropes. Far below, waves crash against the rocks, the spray reaching up toward her toes. She looks up at the guide, firmly gripping the rope, and then beyond his firm stance to the anchor hammered into the cliff side. With a firm push, her legs propel her beyond the ledge and out into space, dropping toward the sea.

Of course she trusts the guide. His strong grip, years of experience, skill, and familiarity with the landscape go a long way in convincing her that she will belay safely to the bottom of the cliff. But it's the rock, pierced by the anchor, which gains her deepest faith. The rock will not fail, will not crumble, and will never falter under her weight.

As we leap, sometimes stumbling, along the cliffs of life, who can we trust? God our Father offers us an anchor in Jesus Christ, who overcame death and is the only hope we have. We can jump with ease from any height, knowing that his strong arms of love will surround us and that our destiny is sure. Our faith grows stronger in this truth: we share in the glory of Jesus through his death and resurrection.

Are you willing to fall, knowing that Jesus is holding the rope? Have you had to really trust God lately? How did you place your faith and hope in him?

He Is Faithful

Your lovingkindness, O LORD, extends to the heavens,
Your faithfulness reaches to the skies.

Psalm 36:5 NASB

Few love stories demonstrate a higher level of faithfulness than that depicted by the life of Hosea the prophet. He was given what seemed to be a very unfair task—to take a prostitute as a wife and commit to loving her. He would watch as his wife and the mother of his children chose to leave the family and return to her life of prostitution. But it didn't end there. Hosea went in search of his wife, and finding her in her debauchery, he *paid* to bring her back home with him—guilty, broken, and dirty.

It would seem a romantic tale of undying love had it happened naturally. However, this story is even more inconceivable when considering that Hosea walked into it with his eyes wide open. Hosea's choice to obey God in spite of what he would suffer is beyond admirable.

It sounds oddly familiar, doesn't it? Jesus, commissioned by the Father, pursued us until we decided to become *his*. But we just can't seem to keep ourselves out of the mess of this world. Jesus doesn't quit. He comes for us again. The price he paid to restore our relationship was his life. He gave up everything to bring us home. That is faithfulness in its fullest measure.

How does your unfaithfulness cause you to doubt the faithfulness of God? Do you know how precious you are to the Father? His faithfulness toward you cannot be exhausted. Let yourself believe it today.

He Makes Me Brave

When you lie down, you will not be afraid;
Yes, you will lie down and your sleep will be sweet.
Do not be afraid of sudden terror,
Nor of trouble from the wicked when it comes;
For the Lord will be your confidence,
And will keep your foot from being caught.

Proverbs 3:24-26 NKJV

A pilot watches the flashing red light. A mother searches frantically for her child between the aisles. A driver glances in the rearview mirror at an oncoming truck. Certain fears have a gripping embrace, paralyzing to the body. The heart pounds, pupils dilate, palms sweat.

Other fears overwhelm the mind, causing anxious thoughts and sleepless nights. How will the bills get paid this month? Will the doctor have bad news? Family members need help, friends are overwhelmed with suffering, and we can't make it all okay.

When fearful thoughts flood our minds, God's words of wisdom and comfort can get washed away. If we can learn to fully trust him, he will calm our fears and still our quickened hearts. We can be fearless because our confidence is in God and his promises.

What fears are holding you captive today? Let the flood of terror subside
and be assured that God is your refuge. He lovingly attends to your
every need. Do not be afraid!

He Forgives Me

What is causing the quarrels and fights among you? Don't they come
from the evil desires at war within you? You want what you don't have,
so you scheme and kill to get it. You are jealous of what others have, but
you can't get it, so you fight and wage war to take it away from them.
James 4:1-2 NLT

Temper tantrums are as common for adults as they are for children; they
just look different in action. Children haven't learned to curb the screaming
and stomping vent of frustration or anger, while adults have more restrained
behavior. But the heart is the same, and the reactions stem from the same
provocation.

James cuts right to the heart of sin. We want what we want but we don't have
it, so we throw a tantrum. It's amazing how simple it is! Watch a child and this
truth will play out soon enough. Watch an adult, and it may be more difficult to
discern, but unfortunately it is there in all of us.

Praise God for his amazing grace, which is extended to us for this very reason.
Let us submit to God's forgiveness and draw near to him for his cleansing and
purifying grace. It washes over us, and our tantrums are forgiven. When we
humble ourselves, he promises to exalt us. What more could we want?

Do you see responses in yourself that remind you of a child throwing a
tantrum? God's forgiveness is bigger than all of that. Thank him today for
his mercy and grace. He loves it when you dwell on that.

He Is Strong When I Am Weak

"My grace is sufficient for you, for my power is made perfect in weakness." Therefore I will boast all the more gladly of my weaknesses, so that the power of Christ may rest upon me.

2 Corinthians 12:9 E SV

Do you ever find yourself suddenly aware of your own glaring weaknesses? Aware that, if left up to your own good works, you wouldn't stand a chance of attaining salvation? We should find great comfort in the fact that we are nothing without salvation in Christ Jesus.

Thankfully, God made a way for us to be united with him, despite impatience, selfishness, anger, and pride. God deeply cares for us and patiently sustains us with steady, faithful, and adoring love.

Amazingly, his love even goes beyond this to *embrace* and *transform* our weakness when we yield it to him. Weakness isn't something to be feared or hidden; weakness submitted to God allows the power of Christ to work in and through us.

When we know our weakness, we are more aware of our need for his strength. And we know that he hears our cry for help before we even utter it. When we put ourselves in a position of humility and ask him to be strong where we are weak, he is delighted to help. You don't have to ask a knight in shining armor twice to rescue his princess.

What does it look like to boast in your weaknesses? Prayerfully submit them to God so that, through him, you can be strong. His transformative love is waiting to graciously restore you.

He Is My Freedom

Creation itself will be set free from its bondage to corruption and obtain the freedom of the glory of the children of God.

Romans 8:21 E SV

Some days begin with praises on our lips and a song to God in our hearts. Humility covers us like a velvet cloth, soothing and delicate and gentle. The truth of God plays on repeat: "God is good! God is good! I am free!" and the entire world's darkness cannot interrupt the chorus.

But other days begin by fumbling with the snooze button and forfeiting the chance to meet him in the quiet stillness. Pride, then, is a sneaky companion, pushing and bitter and ugly, and we wonder if we will ever delight with God again. We feel bound.

The ups and downs should be familiar by now, perhaps, but can we ever become accustomed to the holy living side-by-side with our flesh? One glorious day, flesh will give way to freedom, and there will be no side-by-side. Only the holy will remain. This leaves praise on our lips and a song in our hearts, the unending chorus of his goodness, the velvet covering as we sit before his heavenly throne.

Do you know how much God wants you to rest in his presence? He is waiting and faithful and tender. When you spend time with him, there is no need to hide. You can be exactly who you are. You can say everything you want to say. There is freedom in his presence. How does freedom sound to you right now?

He Is My Friend

Here I am! I stand at the door and knock. If anyone hears my voice and
opens the door, I will come in and eat with that person, and they with me.
Revelation 3:20 NIV

God created you for relationship with him just as he created Adam and Eve. He delights in your voice, your laughter, and your ideas. He longs to fellowship with you just as he did with his first son and daughter.

When life gets difficult, do you run to him with your frustrations? When you're overwhelmed with sadness or grief, do you carry your pain to him? In the heat of anger or frustration, do you call on him for freedom? He is a friend that offers all of this to us—and more—in mercy and love. He is worthy of our friendship.

The friendship he offers to us is a gift of immeasurable worth. There is no one like him; indeed, there is none as worthy of our fellowship than God Almighty, our Maker and Redeemer. Train your heart to run first to God with your pain, joy, frustration, and excitement. His friendship will never let you down!

What are you looking for in a "perfect friend"? Write down your criteria,
and then look no further. God's friendship surpasses all expectation.

He Gives Me Grace

He gives more grace. Therefore He says:
"God resists the proud, But gives grace to the humble."

Maybe you've heard stories of people suffering tragedy, or maybe you're living through a tragedy yourself. Either way, if you had been told you would encounter tragedy, you'd probably have thought, *There's no possible way I could go through that*. And you would be right. You couldn't. You couldn't watch a loved one suffer, couldn't handle losing someone close to you, couldn't continue on if your family turned against you. Why? Because you hadn't yet been given the grace to walk through that situation.

Do we really believe that people who go through tragedy and come out stronger on the other side are any different than ourselves? That they are superhuman somehow? They aren't. They just got to a place where they recognized their desperate need for God's grace in their circumstance—and they asked him for it.

God doesn't call us to walk through seasons of difficulty on our own. He desires to pour out his grace on us. When we need more, he'll pour out some more. And still more. His grace is limitless. His only requirement for ample grace is humility. When we stop thinking we can get through life just fine on our own, he stands ready with his grace.

Have you found yourself in a situation that seems far beyond your scope? There's grace for that. Admit your weakness and ask for God's grace. The moment you ask, his grace is yours in the precise measure you need it.

He Guides Me

All the paths of the Lord are steadfast love and faithfulness,
for those who keep his covenant and his testimonies.

Psalm 25:10 ESV

There is a Family Circus cartoon where the son is asked to take out the garbage. The drawing then traces the tangled and erratic pathway between the boy and his final destination. He bounces over couches, through windows, under wheelbarrows, around trees, between siblings, all on the way to the curbside trash can.

Our lives can feel like this at times: unpredictable, illogical, and inconsistent. Changes in work, marriage, family, or church can make the road seem irrational, uneven, and confusing. But God makes us the promise of a steadfast path when we keep his covenant. When we consider our lives through our limited human perspective, the path seems wavering. But the guidance of Jesus Christ is, in fact, steadfast!

Your path has been chosen for you and your feet have been set upon it. Truly, it is a path of love and faithfulness. He has made a covenant with you and you keep it when you trust him—even in the refinement of your path. It will be uncomfortable at times and you might ask yourself why his guidance is winding you around in the craziest of directions, but trust him! His paths are perfect.

How do you recognize God's faithful leading even though your path
might feel a little uncertain?

He Is My Healer

"Daughter, your faith has made you well; go in peace and be healed of your affliction."

Mark 5:34 NASB

The woman in the crowd had suffered for more than a decade. All of her money had been spent on doctors, but instead of finding healing she was worse than ever. She had one hope, and she reached for it as Jesus passed by her in the crowd. She believed that just a touch, not even from his holy hand but from his garment alone, would bring the healing she desired.

In his brief but blessed response, we hear Jesus' heart for his ailing child: *Daughter, I love your faith! You came to the right place for healing; I know everything about you and the pain you have suffered. Because you have believed in my love for you, you are healed! Be at peace.*

Often, we become fixated on doctoring our own wounds so we can make it through the day. They may be physical, emotional, mental, or spiritual and we may have tried every possible means to treat them. Why not turn instead to the one who can fully repair us? To the one who knows the temperature of our faith in him, rather than just diagnosing our present and burdensome afflictions? Only faith will give us the peace we need to go forward.

He calls you daughter. He knows your burdens, and he wants your faith to be in him and his goodness. What are you seeking healing from today? Put your faith in his goodness and be made whole.

He Is My Hope

There is surely a future hope for you,
and your hope will not be cut off.

Proverbs 23:18 NIV

Abraham took God at his word. Everything about his present circumstance made the idea that he would have a son ridiculous. His body was as good as dead. His own wife laughed at the thought that she, a woman of ninety, body worn out and barren, would nurse a child of her own.

And yet, God had said it—this God that could give life even to the dead and who could call into existence things that didn't yet exist. Abraham would have a son. More than that, his descendants would one day be as numerous as the stars in the sky. Abraham was fully convinced that God was able to do what he promised even when it looked impossible.

Hope starts with the promises of God. When doubt, discouragement, or despair threatens your soul, take heart. We have a God that has already spoken words of life and certainty that will prove to both revive and carry us. Hope is taking God at his Word, believing that all he has said is sure. We have this hope as a trustworthy anchor for the soul (see Hebrews 6:19), allowing us to confidently expect that God will do all he has said he will do.

Which promise from God's Word will you choose to believe this week?

He Is My Inspiration

The precepts of the Lord are right,
giving joy to the heart.
The commands of the Lord are radiant,
giving light to the eyes.

Psalm 19:8 NIV

Children often wonder about the face of God, imagining what he looks like and how his voice might sound. *I want to see God! Where is he?* Where, indeed, beloved?

God is in the beauty, showing off for you. When you see something lovely, you are seeing your Daddy's handiwork. When you hold a newborn baby, and look up and marvel, "I see God!" truly, God is there. Yes, he has created something miraculous, and the miracle inspires his creation.

It's an amazing circle, this inspiration. He gives us so many good gifts—vibrant colors, bursting flavors, comforting warmth, moving melodies, and unimaginable beauty—that our hearts cannot help but respond. And our inspirations pour out in a beautiful offering of worship back to our Creator.

Even his commands, his laws, and his guidance are inspiring! Described as right and radiant, his acts of loving and devoted instructions keep us safe. They also draw us nearer to our Father and give joy and light.

Can you prayerfully submit to God's leadership and the lovely gifts he has planned for you? Let him be your inspiration and see him in the beauty all around you. Don't let his handiwork go unnoticed!

He Knows Me by Name

Lord, you know everything there is to know about me.
You've examined my innermost being With your loving gaze.
You perceive every movement of my heart and soul,
And understand my every thought Before it even enters my mind.
You are so intimately aware of me, Lord,
You read my heart like an open book
And you know all the words I'm about to speak
Before I even start a sentence! You know every step I will take,
Before my journey even begins!

Psalm 139:1-4 TPT

There are people who are terrible with names. And then there are parents. They address you by every name in the household—quite possibly including the dog—all while looking you in the eye... and they gave you the name in the first place!

Chances are, if your name is Mary, Elizabeth, Sara, or Rachel, you've met someone with the same name. There may be thousands of people with *your* name, or there might just be a handful. Either way, it makes no difference to God. He knows you fully. He doesn't take a stab in the dark when you are approaching him, guessing a name and hoping he gets it right. He knows exactly who you are and why you are coming to him. He knows why you've stayed away for so long. He knows your deepest need, your most painful wound, and your darkest thoughts. And still he loves you.

Listen to God as he calls out, "My daughter, beloved one, I know you." How does hearing that you are intimately known by God bring you comfort?

He Is My Joy

Be truly glad. There is wonderful joy ahead.
You love him even though you have never seen him.
Though you do not see him now, you trust him;
and you rejoice with a glorious, inexpressible joy.

1 Peter 1:6, 8 NLT

Life is full of pain and sorrow. Jesus, described as a man of sorrows and acquainted with grief, was no stranger to mourning, weeping, and at one point even declared in agony that he was sorrowful unto death. Jeremiah cried out that his heart was sick within him and his sadness could not be healed. Paul carried burdens so far beyond his strength that he despaired of life. David's pain groans off the pages of the psalms, and Job went so far as to say he wished he had died at birth.

Can joy be found within the piercing anguish of loss? The purest form of joy is often experienced in the arms of sorrow. Joy flows in the middle of the darkness as we trust in God's perfect ways, whispering through our tears, "Not my will, but yours be done."

Joy is clinging to our Savior with the knowledge that Jesus is still who he says he is, even when our pain feels overwhelming. Joy is going to the cross of Christ to sustain us, to give us hope, and to receive his grace and mercy for the days ahead. Delighting in the Lord in the midst of heartache doesn't only produce joy. It *is* joy.

Which circumstance in your life is giving you the opportunity to experience joy in the Lord even as you walk through difficulty?

He Is Just

He did not retaliate when he was insulted, nor threaten revenge when he suffered.
He left his case in the hands of God, who always judges fairly.

1 Peter 2:23 NLT

Our parents were right: life's not fair. We probably learned that first when we didn't get the larger half of the cookie, or when one of our siblings got to go somewhere special while we were at school. As we got older, we might have learned about the lack of fairness a little more harshly: perhaps through wrongful accusations, denied promotions, or unmet expectations.

We hear about big trials, read about complicated court cases, and watch movies dedicated to the theme of *justice*. But many times even after a verdict is reached, the truth is uncertain. It's all about how the case was fought—who had the best lawyers and the most money. Has justice truly been served?

It's easy to be disappointed with the *unfairness* of life. When wrongfully accused or misunderstood, it's hard not to take it to heart. We either want to defend our reputation until the bitter end, or disappear. When faced with these situations, we can rest in the knowledge that God is just. He will judge everyone fairly—not by appearance, false evidence, or hearsay (Isaiah 11:3, TLB).

We don't have to worry about our accusers fighting their case more convincingly. We don't leave our judgment in the hands of a jury. Even the most expensive defense attorney can't make a case against us that will last into eternity. God knows what happened, and, more importantly, he knows our hearts.

How does knowing that God is a fair judge help you let go of your need to defend yourself?

He Is Kind

The LORD directs the steps of the godly.
He delights in every detail of their lives.
Though they stumble, they will never fall,
for the LORD holds them by the hand.

Psalm 37:23-24 NLT

Holding hands is a beautiful act when done in love. We might hold hands with a child to cross the street, to help an aging stranger off of the bus, or to embrace even the smallest part of our beloved while strolling through the park. We grasp hands for a moment, and give safety, kindness, or affection through the simple act.

Can you imagine that God's hand in this same act is extended to those who put their faith in him? Surely his sons and daughters need the spiritual comfort, guidance, and fellowship of God's hand more than any other. And we can be certain that God delights in extending his hand to us as well.

Take comfort in this kindness: God is a caring Father and leads us rightly. We cannot fall when we follow his lead because his loving grip will never let us go. As children trust the hand that leads them safely across the busy street, so we can trust God's kindness. He is gentle, thoughtful, and compassionate, delighting over us.

Can you say yes to his hand, extended gently to you? Will you walk with him, soak in his presence, and share his kindness?

He Gives Me Life

"I am the resurrection and the life. He who believes in me, though he may die, he shall live."

John 11:25 NKJV

Do you want to know a secret? The world has been lying to us. It says, "Eat, drink, and be merry, because tomorrow you will die." It says, "Seize the day for pleasure; it might be the only one you have left!" But this is only a half-truth, a deception of God's Word that gives birth to flesh and sin instead of life and hope.

The truth is that we will live forever. Whether in heaven or hell, we will exist for all eternity. It is because of *this* truth that we must seize the day. Not because we fear our own death, which leads to light, but because we fear the death of those walking in darkness. Death has been sold as being the end of everything, but it is only the end of opportunities to put our trust in Jesus Christ.

It's said that for those who don't have salvation in Jesus Christ, this side of life has the greatest happiness they will ever experience; for followers of Jesus, it has the least. It will only get better when we are face to face with our Savior, through whom we have hope, joy, peace, and the comfort of eternal light.

As you go about your day, find people to share the truth with. Be the light in the darkness, that they too might receive eternal life in Jesus! How can you embrace the truth that the best is yet to come?

He Is Love

We love because he first loved us. If anyone says, "I love God," and hates his brother, he is a liar; for he who does not love his brother whom he has seen cannot love God whom he has not seen.

1 John 4:19-20 E SV

God's greatest commandments are to love him and to love one another. Loving him may come easy; after all, he is patient and loving himself. But the second part of his command can be difficult because it means loving intrusive neighbors at the backyard barbecue, offensive cousins at Christmas dinner, rude cashiers at the grocery store check-out, and insufferable guests who have stayed one night too many in the guestroom.

Loving one another is only possible when we love like him. When we love out of our humanity, sin gets in the way. Obeying the command to love begins with *his* love. When we realize how great his love is for us—how undeserved, unending, and unconditional—we are humbled because we didn't earn it. But he gives it anyway, freely and abundantly, and this spurs us on to love others.

We represent Jesus Christ to the world through love, and we love to the degree that we understand his love for us. If we know how high and wide and deep and long his love is for us, then we have no choice but to pour out that love on others. The intrusive becomes welcome, the offensive becomes peaceful, rudeness gives way to grace, and the insufferable is overshadowed by the cross and all that Jesus suffered there. He did it for all of us; he did it for love.

How can you show love to the unlovely?

He Is All I Need

Happy are those who do not follow the advice of the wicked,
or take the path that sinners tread, or sit in the seat of scoffers;
but their delight is in the law of the Lord,
and on his law they meditate day and night.
They are like trees planted by streams of water,
which yield their fruit in its season, and their leaves do not wither.
In all that they do, they prosper.

Psalm 1:1-3 NRSV

Thanks to a modern diet of technology and social media, women today can feast on heaping portions of gossip, envy, boastful pride, and selfishness. It is not a nourishing diet, but it is deviously sweet. What sicknesses are we susceptible to when we replace time with our Father with time in front of a screen?

Praise God for his nourishment! His Word is as relevant for us today as it was for David thousands of years ago.

Meditate on these words, and hear his voice calling to you. When we spend time with him and read his Word, he is the path to joy and delight. Under his nourishment we yield delicious fruit without the threat of withering. We prosper!

Are you underfed on God's Word? Malnourished from overeating at the modern-day buffet of social media and entertainment? Ask God for his direction. Is a diet overhaul in order? Or a detox of unhealthy habits? He is all you need, no matter what the world puts on the menu!

How important is screen time to you? Can you see how it can
sometimes take away from the abundance of joy, peace, and comfort
found in God's Word?

He Is My Peace

"The Advocate, the Holy Spirit, whom the Father will send in my name, will teach you all things and will remind you of everything I have said to you. Peace I leave with you; my peace I give you. I do not give to you as the world gives. Do not let your hearts be troubled and do not be afraid."

John 14:26-27 NIV

Peace is much-desired but often elusive. Just when we seem to be getting life under control, a new disaster strikes. Just when we find enough calm to settle our minds, a bigger calamity arises. Or worse, the waves of difficulty come one after another with no end in sight.

Those in the armed forces know what it's like to feel one barrage after another and then experience a silence that cannot be trusted. It leads to another onslaught, persistent fighting, and ongoing upheaval. Will there ever be an end to our conflicts? Why does peace elude us?

We find everything we need when we look to God's Word.

The peace begged for on bumper stickers will always elude the world; the peace of Jesus Christ is the only lasting peace, the only true peace that we can attain while walking this earth. Because he knew our weak flesh, Jesus promised us a path to his peace even in this world of struggle—our Advocate, the Holy Spirit.

Do you trust in the peace of God? Is your heart troubled or afraid? Ask the Holy Spirit to give you the peace Jesus promised, and believe that he will accomplish what this conflicted world cannot.

He Gives Me Endurance

Let us throw off everything that hinders and the sin that so easily
entangles. And let us run with perseverance the race marked out for us,
fixing our eyes on Jesus... so that you will not grow weary and lose heart.
Hebrews 12:1-3 NIV

There is no such thing as "retirement" for those who serve God. There won't be a spiritual pension waiting for us so that we can finally relax and let others finish God's good work. We might have travel ideas, plans to focus on a hobby, or dreams of unwinding and living easy while everyone else labors away, but God doesn't stop using us!

Our prayers, testimonies, encouragement, wisdom, and faith must never retire from use. Bringing glory to the kingdom of God is a full-time effort requiring long-term endurance. While we wait to enjoy that glory, God has plans that aren't put off by our aging bodies. We are encouraged to continue on without interruption. We are promised those beautiful words of approval, "Well done, good and faithful servant!" upon the completion of our earthly journey.

In case you have doubts, know this: it will be worth it! Will you falter? Slow down to refuel? Take rest during seasons of fatigue? Perhaps. But keep your eyes fixed on his. You might run. You might crawl. You might move mere inches per day. But if you remove the tangles of sin and keep your eyes fixed on him, you won't grow weary and lose heart. This is his promise.

You can't retire yet. He will remain at your side every step of the way,
until you bask in the full glory of the only paradise worth persevering for!
How does this help you endure through the struggles of life?

He Hears My Prayers

Why am I praying like this? Because I know you will answer me, O God!
Yes, listen as I pray.

Psalm 17:6 TLB

There are those days when words fail us. We can barely string a coherent sentence together, let alone articulate exactly what we need. Grief has found us and it seems to have taken over our ability to think, or speak, or pray. Tears roll silently down our cheeks, our hearts ache, and still no words come.

Be encouraged. Not only does God *hear* your prayers when they tumble clumsily from your lips, he knows what you need prior to you asking (Matthew 6:8). He's aware of what you require to get through today before you can put it into words. And when you do finally put words to your thoughts that seem completely inadequate? It doesn't matter. God heard your heart.

Your prayers, no matter how unintelligible they seem to you (or others), are heard and understood by God. Let your heart be filled with peace as you silently acknowledge your need for him. Your message to God is not lost in translation. He interprets it perfectly every time. How does this encourage you to keep praying?

He Is My Protection

Let all who take refuge in you be glad;
let them ever sing for joy.
Spread your protection over them,
that those who love your name may rejoice in you.

Psalm 5:11 NIV

Huddled in the basement of the museum, visitors waited for the hurricane to pass. Children cried or slept, parents' expressions were tight and anxious. Museum staff held walkie-talkies and flashlights, beams bouncing nervously. Sirens wailed, winds howled, and the depths of the shelter shook as the mighty storm raged outside.

Even with modern engineering advancements implemented, those sheltered from the storm were worried. There was no guarantee of safety. Could we expect the huddled crowds to be singing for joy? Rejoicing in their place of refuge? If they were aware of the one who has promised to always protect, then their praises would echo off of the shelter walls!

In the shadow of God's protection we can be glad. He is the only one able to guarantee our safety! His protection spreads over us, stronger than any bomb shelter or apocalyptic bunker we could engineer.

Can you relate to this need for protection today? Imagine delighting through the storm, singing while the structures come crashing down, knowing all the while that you are standing under the mighty hand of God.

He Provides for Me

Because of our faith, Christ has brought us into this place of undeserved
privilege where we now stand, and we confidently and joyfully look
forward to sharing God's glory.

Romans 5:2 NLT

Pull up to the drive-through, place an order for the coffee that will help start the day, and hear the cashier's words, "Your order was paid for by the car in front of you." This unexpected generosity gives birth to humbling gratitude, and the day is now overcome with God's presence. A stranger may have been the instrument of kind provision, but the inspiration is unmistakable.

God is the author of generosity, providing us with all we need. Look at all he gave to Adam and Eve, and how little he asked for in return! They walked in his presence daily, enjoying authentic relationship with their Father. *Just don't eat the fruit from that tree or you will die.* Even when they ate it, God provided atonement for them.

We, like Adam and Eve, have sinned and deserve death. But Christ is our substantial provision! As if eternity in his kingdom weren't enough, he blesses us each and every day, whether we acknowledge it or not. Some things, like free coffee at the drive-through, are small provisions. Others are subtle or unseen altogether. But he is working his love out in generous portions for you, his beloved!

In what ways have you seen God generously provide for you lately?

He Is Pure

Teach me your ways, O LORD,
that I may live according to your truth!
Grant me purity of heart,
so that I may honor you.

Psalm 86:11 NLT

If you've ever tried to clean a white dog who had decided to run around in the mud, you'll know it seems like an impossible task to get rid of every speck of dirt—especially if said puppy isn't too keen on the bathing procedure. If it could just sit and allow its owner to work carefully and methodically, all traces of dirt could likely be eliminated. But often neither the dog nor its owner has that kind of patience.

Cleaning up the sin in our lives can feel similar. Finding and ridding ourselves of all impurity can be a slow and painful process. It might seem downright impossible at times. Maybe we don't want to be examined, or perhaps sitting still is the problem.

The good news is we don't have to try to purify ourselves. We allow God to do it for us. Fortunately, he is patient, and he has the perfect solution. He uses the sacrifice of his Son—the pure, spotless lamb—to wash away all of our dirt. Every last speck.

Does the thought of being thoroughly cleaned appeal to you, or does it make you nervous? Maybe the answer is a little of both. You can trust your Master to gently wash all the filth away and cause you to be pure again. Can you sit still for long enough to let him do it?

He Gives Me Purpose

The LORD will fulfill his purpose for me;
your steadfast love, O LORD, endures forever.
Do not forsake the work of your hands.

Psalm 138:8 ESV

Life often doesn't turn out the way we think it should. When we're stuck in the midst of circumstances we never wanted—dreams lost and hope buried—it's difficult to find meaning in it all, and it can seem impossible to keep going.

But God gives purpose to our pain and hope to carry on.

Hardships provide a distinct opportunity for the Lord to mold us more into his image. Hardships compel the God-loving souls to hold on to their God solely because of who he is, not just because of what he can give.

When it feels a lot more like we're surviving in him rather than actively abiding in him, he comforts us with the promise that he will complete the work he began in us, making all things beautiful in his time. We have the blessing of embracing all that is going on in our lives as part of his trustworthy plan to glorify himself and to accomplish his loving intentions for us.

How have you seen God mold you more into the image of Jesus through painful circumstances? What hope does the promise of a fulfilled purpose bring you?

He Heals My Broken Relationships

Draw near to God, and he will draw near to you. Cleanse your hands, you sinners, and purify your hearts, you double-minded. Do not speak evil against one another, brothers. The one who speaks against a brother or judges his brother, speaks evil against the law and judges the law.

James 4:8, 11 ESV

We were created for relationship. Since Adam expressed the need for a companion, people have sought fellowship together. But no matter how strong our desire to have healthy, loving relationships, it can be hard to move past the pain of a broken one. It may be a divorce, an estranged sister or mother, or a longtime friend who has somehow become a bitter rival. In order for reconciliation to take place, we must look to God for direction.

First, pray. Submit yourself to God and refuse to allow the enemy any further destruction. Next, ask him what sin, if any, you have committed to contribute to the dissent. Confess it, repent, and let it go. Now comes the hard part: don't speak out against them. Don't slander or gossip or share your grievance; it won't make things better. In fact, it only makes things worse.

Can you extend forgiveness instead of judgment? Let the love of God flow through you and onto those you are at odds with. Begin to pray daily for reconciliation and restoration. God is your healer and he wants this relationship to be restored more than you do!

He Is My Redeemer

"The Spirit of the Lord is upon me,
because he has anointed me
to proclaim good news to the poor.
He has sent me to proclaim liberty to the captives
and recovering of sight to the blind,
to set at liberty those who are oppressed,
to proclaim the year of the Lord's favor."

Luke 4:18-19 ESV

When Jesus, the long awaited Messiah, revealed his deity to his family, his disciples, and the crowds, they were expecting a mighty king who would deliver them from their oppressors and establish his everlasting kingdom. What they got was a humble servant who dined with tax collectors and whose feet were cleansed by the tears of a prostitute. Jesus wasn't exactly what they thought he would be.

He was better! He came to bring salvation to those who were drowning in a sea of sin and sickness; those who were cast out and in need of holy redemption; those whom the religious leaders had deemed unworthy but whose hearts longed for true restoration. He came to redeem his people, but not in the way they expected.

Jesus delivers you from the bonds of sin and oppression through his
death and resurrection and through your repentance from sin by faith.
The Spirit of the Lord is upon you and he has anointed you! Proclaim this
good news today; you have been set free!

He Brings Refreshment

"The water I give them," he said, "becomes a perpetual spring within them, watering them forever with eternal life."

John 4:13-14 TLB

Have you ever been so thirsty you thought you'd never be able to take in enough water to quench your thirst? Maybe you've been somewhere so hot you were sure you would jump in a dirty puddle just to cool off. Imagine stumbling upon an oasis in the middle of the desert or a crystal clear swimming hole at the bottom of a waterfall in the jungle. How refreshing that would be!

The word *refreshment* itself sounds like a cool drink for the weary soul. The Bible says, "The law of the LORD is perfect, refreshing the soul" (Psalm 19:7, NIV). God's Word is our source of life and energy. It gives us what we so desperately need, and it's available all the time! If you spend time in the Scriptures, you'll find his Word is *in* you, waiting to revitalize and invigorate you.

God's Word will never run dry. His water is life-giving and eternal—refreshing! That *perpetual spring* is in you ready to be drawn upon at any moment of the day or night. What an encouragement that is when we are tired, frustrated, sad, or confused.

In what areas of your life do you sense a need for refreshment? Spend time in the Word of God and find that long, cool drink you are looking for.

He Gives Me Rest

"So everyone, come to me! Are you weary, carrying a heavy burden? Then come to me. I will refresh your life, for I am your oasis. Simply join your life with mine. Learn my ways and you'll discover that I'm gentle, humble, easy to please. You will find refreshment and rest in me. For all that I require of you will be pleasant and easy to bear."

Matthew 11:28-30 TPT

There are times when grief leaves you bone tired. The thought of doing even the most simple task seems overwhelming. Getting out of bed, getting dressed, cooking dinner, or taking kids to practice become insurmountable chores. The world continues to spin, and you can think of nothing you'd like better than to stop and get off for a while. Trying to keep up with life's demands feels impossible.

So don't try.

Admit your weakness and ask God for his strength. You will find that he is very resourceful when you allow him to be. Someone shows up on your doorstep with dinner? Accept it. That was a gift of rest from God. A friend swings by to pick up your kids for practice? Say thank you. That was God, too.

Accepting that we need help can sometimes be the hardest part. Once we let go of the need to appear as if everything is ok, we are in a better position to receive help. How do you feel knowing that God is gentle, humble, and easy to please? Can you find your refreshment and rest in him today?

He Makes All Things New

Bless the Lord, O my soul, and forget not all his benefits,
who forgives all your iniquity, who heals all your diseases,
who redeems your life from the pit,
who crowns you with steadfast love and mercy,
who satisfies you with good
so that your youth is renewed like the eagle's.

Psalm 103:2-5 ESV

Is it reasonable to believe that a marathon runner can finish a race without a single replenishing cup of water? Would it be fair to expect a doctor, after working a 36-hour shift, to have the energy to perform one last tedious surgery? Can a child be expected not to lick the spatula that mixed the cookie dough? Should a foreigner be familiar with the customs of a new land?

We know that humans have limits. We need to eat and drink regularly. We get tired and cranky if we don't have enough sleep. We learn patience and self-control as we get older, and our emotions can be overwhelmed by life's great upheavals. The shepherd king, David, knew this and understood God's gracious and loving path of renewal.

Whether you are at peak performance or running on empty, needing renewal now or in the future, God alone can give you what you need for renewal of your mind, body, spirit, and strength because he knows your limits and capabilities. He knows that you need time to refuel, space to recover your strength, and that sometimes a little cookie dough goes a long way.

Be renewed today. Don't believe that you are weak because you need to rest; you aren't meant to be strong forever. You are designed to lean on the one whose strength can renew you. Tell him how much you need him today!

He Restores My Soul

"Stop wailing," Jesus said. "She is not dead but asleep." They laughed at him, knowing that she was dead. But he took her by the hand and said, "My child, get up!" Her spirit returned, and at once she stood up. Then Jesus told them to give her something to eat.

Luke 8:52-55 NIV

Do you know *whose* you are? Your father and mother rightly claim you as their child, but do you recognize Jesus as the one who restores you as his daughter? He knows your coming and going, your every inner working; you are *his*.

How difficult it is to put our needs into the hands of the Father! Do we dare hope? Imagine watching your child die and feeling the despair of her absence, only to have Jesus claim that she is asleep. Both the girl's father and Jesus loved the child; both claimed her as their daughter. But only Jesus commanded her spirit and her life. His child hears his voice and obeys his command; she gets up and is restored!

God is faithful to the deepest needs of your heart; he knows you full well! Where is he directing you today? Are you a daughter in need of healing? Of hope? Hear his voice and let your spirit be renewed!

He Is My Reward

"I will bring the blind by a way they did not know;
I will lead them in paths they have not known.
I will make darkness light before them, And crooked places straight.
These things I will do for them, And not forsake them."

Isaiah 42:16 NKJV

Spring is a time of rebirth and renewal, a reward for making it through the long, cold, desolate winter. Some parts of the world have enjoyed colorful spring gardens in full fragrant bloom for weeks. In other regions, the cold snow is still melting and the earliest bulbs have yet to reach through the hard soil. Whether above the surface or below, resurrection is happening all around us, rewarding us with new life and vitality.

When this happens around you, let the joy lead you to the empty tomb, where Jesus' miraculous resurrection also brings new life. Resurrection is a revival of hope, of light shining in the darkness, of our glorious reward.

Isaiah 42:16 shares a promise that cannot be taken away from us. He has achieved his glory and we will share in its reward: death cannot conquer or steal our inheritance! Therefore, we can fully trust and believe in Jesus Christ, our hope. There is nothing more magnificent, nothing else worthy of our expectations, for he has made a way for us to share in his glory!

Let the sins that have hindered you melt away like the winter snow, and allow his renewing strength to overwhelm your soul. Breathe in this fresh start. Today is a new day, full of promise and life. Receive the reward of salvation as a gift. How can you let what is gone pass away, and look with hope to the resurrection of Christ Jesus and the new day that rises?

He Is My King

So that we would know for sure that we are his true children, God released the Spirit of Sonship into our hearts—moving us to cry out intimately, "My Father! You're our true Father!" Now we're no longer living like slaves under the law, but we enjoy being God's very own sons and daughters! And because we're his, we can access everything our Father has.

Galatians 4:6-7 TPT

Picture a beautiful white castle perched on a mountain top overlooking a crystal-clear lake surrounded by trees. Decadent turrets and towers reach high into the sky, affording a breathtaking view to all who are privileged enough to enter. High walls, a watchtower, and open parapets ensure maximum protection from enemy forces. Inside, vaulted ceilings and crystal chandeliers tower above sprawling staircases. Ornate sculptures and paintings grace the walls, and the grand hall echoes with laughter.

The King appears. For a moment, you tremble, unsure of how to respond. Then, as he advances toward you with arms wide open, you remember—*this is my Daddy. And this is my home.* You run as fast as you can into those arms, and lose yourself in his warm embrace.

It sounds like a fairytale, but that picture doesn't even do justice to the home or the Father awaiting us. Gold, silver, sparkling jewels, decadence, opulence, splendor, immeasurable love, joy, peace, and unbroken relationship—it's our inheritance! The King of all kings calls us his children. That means we are royalty, and everything he has he wants to share with us.

In this life we *will* have troubles. We will suffer; we will hurt. But the promise of eternity with our majestic King and all he has created is more than worth it.

Today, revel in the eternity that awaits you. How does it give you hope in the midst of your present circumstances?

He Is My Hiding Place

*Wherever I am, though far away at the ends of the earth, I will cry to you
for help. When my heart is faint and overwhelmed, lead me to the mighty,
towering Rock of safety. For you are my refuge, a high tower where my
enemies can never reach me.*

Psalm 61:2-3 TLB

When emotional injuries—insecurities, anxieties, memories of abuse, conflict,
or pain—that were buried long ago come to the surface of life, they transform
from past scars to raw, gaping wounds, brand new and scorching. Earthly
bandages cannot completely heal the pain. We need God's touch, the balm of
his tenderness, upon us. It aches, but he is a safe hiding place—a refuge when we
are afraid to walk through the pain.

Abiding in his safety and leaving the wound open is the hardest part. We have
to see it, feel it, and let God walk us through the healing process. And that might
take time. But he is a loving, worthy, compassionate Father, whose treatment
roots out all infection and disease so that the scars can remain healed. We are
safe when we are in his care, and he promises to protect us.

Do you believe that you are precious to him? That he loves you with a fiercely
protective, eternally faithful, inescapable love? He is true and worthy and invites
you to bring him all of your hurts, pains, regrets, and brokenness so he can put it
back together.

*Will you take refuge in his arms? Will you submit your wounds to his
careful attention?*

He Satisfies Me

O my dove, in the clefts of the rock,
in the crannies of the cliff,
let me see your face,
let me hear your voice,
for your voice is sweet,
and your face is lovely.

Song of Solomon 2:14 E SV

Stress threatens to get the better of us, and sometimes we just want to hide. Remembering that secret bar of chocolate in the pantry, we may scurry off to do just that: bury ourselves away with the temporary but sweet comfort that helps the world slow down, if only for a moment.

The same instinct can arise with God. We get overwhelmed by his ministry or overdue for his forgiveness or out of touch with his Word and lose track of who he is. Instead of running toward him, we hide from him and look for other ways to meet our needs. We cannot hide from him, and in love he calls out to us.

We cannot outrun his love for us, nor should we try. Instead, let's leave the false safety of the clefts and crannies and pantries with hidden chocolate.

Feel the pleasure of his friendship: this God who wants to hear your voice and see your face because he finds them sweet and lovely. Is there anyone else who can satisfy you so perfectly?

He Is My Security

In peace I will lie down and sleep,
for you alone, LORD,
make me dwell in safety.

Psalm 4:8 NIV

Have you ever spent hours—or minutes that seemed like hours—searching frantically for Blankie, Paci, or Lambie in an attempt to quiet the inconsolable child sprawled on the floor? Ah, that wonderful security item. The magic silencer. The instant peace maker. The middle-of-the-night sanity that we are willing to fumble around in the dark for.

As kids grow older, we try to wean them off those security items: the blankets that are torn to shreds, the teddy bears with missing eyes, or the pacifiers that are chewed beyond recognition. Most children don't agree that they could do without the security of those things—and they have a point.

Think of all the times you've walked through trials and found yourself at a loss. Where do you go to feel secure? The best place you can go is to God. He is our security, and he gives us the strength we need to press on. We should feel lost when we don't have him nearby. When he's right beside us—sharing our pillow in the dark of night, riding beside us in the car, or sitting next to us at our desk— we sense that everything is going to be ok.

Don't look anywhere else for your security. Find it in God.

How does it look to have God as your security? What do you need to trust him with today?

He Is Always In Control

Do not be anxious about anything, but in every situation, by prayer and petition, with thanksgiving, present your requests to God. And the peace of God, which transcends all understanding, will guard your hearts and your minds in Christ Jesus.

Philippians 4:6-7 NIV

The counselor's suggestion box overflowed with ideas from the school's young students, varying from inventive and reasonable (replacing fluorescent lights with tons of twinkling Christmas lights) to imaginative but impractical (covering the hallways with giant slip n' slides). But each one was read aloud during weekly staff meetings. The children's ideas never decreased in volume or zeal; they believed that their school could be greater than any other, and that their school counselor not only respected but valued their input.

As a result, students also approached the counselor with their personal troubles; he heard about failures on the soccer field, fights with best friends, botched geometry quizzes, and sibling rivalries. His door was always open, and the seats weren't empty for long. What did he offer these young hearts and minds? What was the secret to giving them serenity in the midst of those tumultuous years? He mimicked the example set by God, our great Counselor, who hears our worries and protects us with his peace.

This is a tried-and-true method: God bends his ear to our anxieties, our longings, our frustrations, and our worship. And we trust him because we want to be better than ever, to be more and more like him. We trust that our Counselor values our petitions.

It may seem difficult to give thanks in the midst of trouble and fear, but when we do, God replaces our worries with peace. We aren't meant to understand how he does it, but we will be guarded against the lies of the enemy. Only in Christ Jesus is this possible.

Will you fill the suggestion box of your wonderful Counselor who is always in control? He will give you his peace!

_____

_____

_____

_____

_____

_____

_____

_____

_____

_____

_____

_____

_____

_____

_____

_____

_____

_____

He Is My Strength

"I will sing to the Lord, for he has triumphed gloriously;
the horse and his rider he has thrown into the sea.
The Lord is my strength and my song,
and he has become my salvation;
this is my God, and I will praise him,
my father's God, and I will exalt him."

Exodus 15:1-2 ESV

Have you ever watched the Olympics and marveled at the incredible strength, discipline, and God-given talent of the athletes? Watching interviews, we commonly hear the question, "Where do you get the strength—the motivation?"

Daily life, while not an Olympic sport, requires its own motivation if we are to push through the blood, sweat, and tears to the gold medal that awaits us. Moses, after the victorious escape from Pharaoh's army, praises the source of their strength in the Scripture above.

Are you facing an Olympic-sized trial? Are you wondering where your strength to endure will come from? Does it seem absolutely crazy that God can and will lift you up to overcome? Remember that he is your strength and your song; trust his power to be yours and praise him because he is worthy. He alone has the strength you need, and he supports you time and time again. Trust him, thank him, exalt him, and the gold medal will be yours!

He Is My Foundation

Let your roots grow down into him, and let your lives be built on him.
Then your faith will grow strong in the truth you were taught, and you
will overflow with thankfulness.

Colossians 2:7 NLT

His brothers laughed at his heavy laboring, day in and day out, while they lounged around. Their homes had taken no time at all to complete, and they liked them just fine. Until the wolf came, with his gusting huffs and puffs and then...

The story is as familiar as its lesson: take the time to do things right so when trouble comes you will be safe. Build with worthy materials, and you'll have something that lasts through the fiercest of storms.

The third brother must've been a God-fearing little pig, as he took the advice that Jesus gave to his followers. Build on the rock and your house will not fall. Build on something shifting, like sand, grass, or sticks, and watch it fall when the rains, floods, and winds come. God is the rock on which we can build with confidence.

Not only can we have assurance in his firm foundation, but he promises to bless us as we dwell with him. Rains, flooding, gusting wind *will* come, but he will see us through every storm with truth which will strengthen our faith. We will see him triumph over sin and darkness and we will overflow with thankfulness!

In the midst of the storms, you can rejoice! As the winds howl around you, your faith will grow strong. Nothing will come against you that can blow your house down when you build it on the strong foundation of Jesus. How have you seen Jesus as your stronghold recently?

He Is My Support

Whom have I in heaven but you?
And earth has nothing I desire besides you.
My flesh and my heart may fail,
but God is the strength of my heart
and my portion forever.

Psalm 73:25-26 NIV

When considering a home remodeling project, it's important to determine where the support beams are. If we just knock a wall down here and there to create more space, it could have a detrimental effect on the rest of the structure. In fact, it could even lead to irreparable damage.

Whether a building topples because of faulty construction, a bad foundation, or extraordinary loads, you can bet the support beams were compromised.

Support beams can be like those people in our lives that we look up to. People we love. People we respect. People we depend on. Sometimes they fall—and we might not realize we were leaning on them until they do. When they go down, it can be hard to recover. They might leave a wake of destruction in their collapse.

The only support beam you can lean on and guarantee it will never shake, bend, or crumble under pressure is God. When the world around you seems to have collapsed, and you find yourself floundering around looking for something firm to take hold of, grab God's hand. He is steady and sure, and his love is safe.

What support beams have you experienced tumbling down around you? Do you know how much the Lord desires to hold you up while everything else crumbles? Ask him to be your support beam today. He is more than enough for your every need.

He Is My All in All

I fall to my knees and pray to the Father, the Creator of everything in heaven and on earth. I pray that from his glorious, unlimited resources he will empower you with inner strength through his Spirit. Then Christ will make his home in your hearts as you trust in him. Your roots will grow down into God's love and keep you strong. And may you have the power to understand, as all God's people should, how wide, how long, how high, and how deep his love is. May you experience the love of Christ, though it is too great to understand fully. Then you will be made complete with all the fullness of life and power that comes from God.

Ephesians 3:14-19 NLT

Gloomy days happen. In the midst of the dreariness it helps to hear the voice of a friend, especially one who points us so perfectly to the sustenance we need. The prayer of Paul, addressed to those in desperate need of hearing the promises of life in Jesus Christ, is a prayer for you.

Pray this for yourself, your friend, your neighbor, your coworker. Pray until you feel the roots deepening and strengthening in love. Pray it again and again until the power to understand overwhelms you—he is all you need! Pray it until the fullness of God's love for you overcomes your gloom. Pray until the life and power of God break through the clouds and shine brightly upon your face. He is all you need. You can trust him for everything!

He Is Always There for Me

God's way is perfect.
All the LORD's promises prove true.
He is a shield for all who look to him for protection.
For who is God except the LORD?
Who but our God is a solid rock?

Psalm 18:30-31 NLT

From famous songs to television commercials to close friends, there's a promise that is often made and rarely kept. *I'm here for you; you can always count on me.* Most of us have promised or been promised this sometime in our life, and most, if not all, have felt that sting of rejection or disappointment when things didn't quite turn out that way.

We say "nobody's perfect," but somehow we expect that everyone should be. In the midst of our trying circumstances, we call out to the people who promised to always be there, but they don't answer. They don't even call us back. Loved ones will hurt us because they are human. Even the best friend, the closest sister, the doting parent will fail in their ability to be there for you. There's no escaping it.

But there is someone who you *can* always count on. You can tell him everything. He listens. He *hears* you. He'll wrap his arms around you, stroke your hair, and tell you everything is going to be all right. God is perfect—the perfect Father, the perfect friend. He is completely trustworthy.

Have you been disappointed or hurt by someone you love? How can you extend grace to them today? Trust in the one who is dependable. God is willing and able to be your solid rock. He is the one you can always turn to.

He Is Truth

Send out your light and your truth;
let them lead me;
let them bring me to your holy hill
and to your dwelling.

Psalm 43:3 NRSV

When we are weak, the enemy may just try to sneak in and pepper us with lies—to kick us while we're down. It's an incredibly effective tactic. Our best line of defense is to surround ourselves with the truth. Read it. Think it. Pray it. Declare it.

In John 1:1, we read that the Word was with God in the beginning, and the Word was God. In Psalm 119:160, it says, "The very essence of your words is truth." Using simple logic, we put these Scriptures together and derive the following: If the Word is God and the Word is truth, then God is truth.

When you find yourself believing the lies of the enemy, turn to God's Word. Find your encouragement, joy, peace, and strength in his never-changing truth. No matter how many lies you have believed in the past, or how many you are believing right now, you can shut that deceptive voice down by saturating yourself in the truth of God's Word.

What lies do you need to expose to God's truth today?

He Understands Me

"My sheep hear my voice, and I know them, and they follow me. I give them eternal life, and they will never perish, and no one will snatch them out of my hand."

John 10:27-28 ESV

An international festival is held each year and the most popular event showcases the talents of Irish sheep dogs. The shepherd uses whistles and quiet voice commands to direct the dog, who in turn herds the sheep through various obstacles and dangers. Audiences marvel at the speed of the dogs and the swift changes in the herd's direction, all due to the effective communication between man, dog, and sheep.

Jesus often spoke about shepherds, calling himself our Good Shepherd. His followers understood that sheep need help through many obstacles and dangers, just as we do. And we need Jesus to communicate with us in a quiet, familiar voice so we will know which way to turn for safety.

Our shepherd has one goal: keep his lambs safe. He hems us in, depending on our destination, with gentle calls and prodding where necessary. He understands our limits, our tendency to wander, our nature to rebel. In his goodness, he nudges our sides, reminding us to trust him and obey his commands. We must follow him to safety, to eternal life.

When you listen to God, moving in unison with speed and accuracy, you are an example to a lost world. Trust and obey, knowing that God understands you and leads you to glory. Let audiences marvel at your Good Shepherd.

Take some time to listen for his voice today. He understands you on a much deeper level than you may know.

He Gives Me Victory

Can anything ever separate us from Christ's love? Does it mean he no longer loves us if we have trouble or calamity, or are persecuted, or hungry, or destitute, or in danger, or threatened with death? No, despite all these things, overwhelming victory is ours through Christ, who loved us.

Romans 8:35, 37 NLT

The Miracle Mop promised to be the solution for every mopping mess. No more stubborn stains, stuck-on grime, or back-breaking scrubbing and scouring. The solution was simple! Only $49.95 and pesky housework is defeated! It's a tempting promise, certainly, but could housekeeping victory really be achieved with a credit card? Such assurances tug at our pocketbooks because...well...life is messy and sometimes a short-cut is downright tantalizing! But we know it's never that easy. The mop doesn't push itself, after all!

It's tempting to take short-cuts, but a life of victory isn't a life without disappointment or hard work. Jesus promised us trials and difficulties as we follow him. This world is a fallen one, full of people using their free-will for sin and destruction. Jesus' promise was meant to prepare us for the rejection, bitterness, and hatred we would encounter.

Jesus also promised us grace, strength, hope, and victory. Don't be deceived to think that good works, prayers, or even faith will produce a life of ease and earthly blessing, showered down from above. We have one promise of victory and that is the saving love of Jesus Christ.

Don't ever fear that you will be overcome; his love, even in times of despair, is victorious over all. Are you willing to scrub and scour? What other promises of victory do you need to shut out? Anything other than Jesus Christ, whose death and resurrection are your great and glorious victory, is a waste of your precious time!

He Makes Me Whole

He will take our weak mortal bodies and change them into glorious bodies like his own, using the same power with which he will bring everything under his control.

Philippians 3:21 NLT

When a flower pot crashes to the pavement or a vase shatters to the floor, we consider the damage in hopes that it can be repaired. What is left? Dangerously tiny shards of glass, too small to piece back together? Or simple, bulky pieces, like those of a puzzle, needing only glue and patience? One thing is certain: we will work harder to fix something that has great value to us.

Just like the broken pottery, we are broken vessels in need of extensive repairs. No elaborate doctoring is required, however, just the humblest of procedures. We hold out our hands and give our broken, desperate, painful, sinful, prideful selves over to the one who mends us into wholeness without a single remaining scar or crack.

How can God do this? Because he is both holy and whole, and we are his creation. We were always meant to be perfect, but sin got in the way. Now, we can only submit to the one whose healing work never leaves a scar and whose abiding love makes us whole forever.

Do you have scars of brokenness that need healing?
Hold everything up to God, who fully covers everything,
and in the process makes you whole.

He Gives Me Wisdom

Listen carefully to wisdom;
set your mind on understanding.
Cry out for wisdom,
and beg for understanding.

Proverbs 2:2-3 NCV

Grief has a funny way of messing with our heads. It can cause a fog to roll in and settle over our minds. Small decisions feel like monstrous ones, or maybe it's the opposite: big decisions are made hastily because, quite frankly, we don't have the energy to think everything through. So how do we get the wisdom we need for the task set before us? We ask God for it.

King Solomon was put in charge of a nation. He knew it was an impossible task to complete without wisdom. He wasn't *born* the wisest man who ever lived; he acquired his wisdom by asking God to give it to him. James 1:5 says that if we lack wisdom, we should also ask God for it. We can be confident that if God tells us to ask for something, he wants to grant that request. If God can give Solomon wisdom to run a kingdom, he can certainly give us wisdom to make decisions about big and small things in our lives.

Sometimes God provides us with sound advice through family members, friends, or counselors. This can be especially important to seek out when we don't feel like we can see through the fog. Other advisors help us gain the perspective we might be lacking. They can assist us in making an informed decision instead of a hasty one.

What do you need wisdom for right now? Don't hesitate to ask God for
understanding. He wants to give it to you if you're willing to listen.